DRAWING MANGA
INSECTS

PowerKiDS press.

New York

Published in 2008 by The Rosen Publishing Group, Inc.
29 East 21st Street, New York, NY 10010

First Edition

American Editor: Rachel O'Connor
Japanese Editorial: Ray Productions
Book Design: Erica Clendening
Coloring: Erica Clendening, Julio Gil, Zachary Grillo, Thomas Somers

Manga: Masaki Nishida

Photo Credits: p. 23 (Ant, Butterfly, Caterpillar, Scorpion, Ladybug, Spider) © Digital Vision; p. 23 (Dragonfly) © Erica Clendening; p. 23 (Bumblebee) © Photodisc.

Library of Congress Cataloging-in-Publication Data

Nishida, Masaki, 1960-
Drawing manga insects / Masaki Nishida.
    p. cm.   \ (How to draw manga)
 Includes index.
 ISBN-13: 978-1-4042-3847-3 (library binding)
 ISBN-10: 1-4042-3847-6 (library binding)
 1. Insects in art \Juvenile literature. 2. Comic books, strips,
etc. \Japan \Technique \Juvenile literature. 3.
Cartooning \Technique \Juvenile literature. I. Title.
 NC1764.8.I57N57 2008
 741.5'1 \dc22
                                    2007002090

Manufactured in the United States of America

CONTENTS

All About Manga

Hello, my name is Sayomi, and I love to read and draw manga. Since I'm a manga artist, I not only draw manga characters, but write and illustrate stories as well. I have drawn many different things, from animals to dinosaurs, and have written stories based on the characters I've created. Being creative is fun, and in the world of manga, anything goes!

In this book you will need the following supplies:

- A **sketch** pad or a single sheet of paper
- A pencil
- A pencil sharpener
- A ballpoint or a fine felt pen
- An eraser
- Your imagination!

My friend Masaki and I will be your guides through this book. We will show you how to draw manga insects step-by-step. Masaki is waiting for you on the next page.

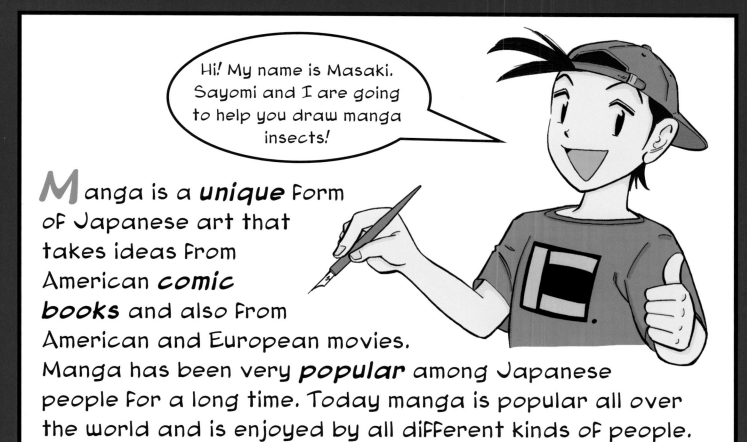

Hi! My name is Masaki. Sayomi and I are going to help you draw manga insects!

Manga is a **unique** form of Japanese art that takes ideas from American **comic books** and also from American and European movies. Manga has been very **popular** among Japanese people for a long time. Today manga is popular all over the world and is enjoyed by all different kinds of people.

People like manga because of the combination of pictures and **text**. It's easy to follow the exciting **plots** of the stories. Unlimited adventures can be created in the manga world. In this book we will show you how to draw eight insects as manga characters. We will then show you examples of stories that can be based on the characters.

This book will teach you how to draw manga insects. We hope that the stories we provide will inspire you to create your own manga stories. Now let's go learn how to draw manga insects and have some fun!

DRAWING AN
ANT

Ants may be small and hard to see, but they are very hard workers.

Are you ready to draw a hard-working ant?

1 Start by drawing an oval for the head.

2 Add three ovals for the chest and the body.

3 Draw six hands and legs with lines and ovals. Don't forget the eyes and mouth.

4 Add in the extra details to the face and body.

5 Ink the lines you want to keep and erase the rest.

6 Finish by coloring. Now your ant is ready to get to work!

THE ANT COLONY

DRAWING A
BUTTERFLY

One of the most beautiful insects you'll see is the butterfly. Let's draw the popular Monarch butterfly.

Draw an oval for the head.

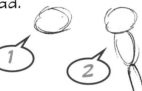

Add two more ovals for the chest and the body.

Add two triangles and two ovals for the wings.

Draw the **antennae**, one pair of hands, and four legs. Add details to the head and wings.

Ink the final lines and erase any pencil lines you don't want to keep.

Add any colors you like. Your butterfly is now ready to fly!

A BUTTERFLY'S TASTE

DRAWING A
CATERPILLAR

You know this caterpillar is the *larvae* of the monarch butterfly, don't you?

I sure do. Let's draw one!

1 Draw an oval for the caterpillar's head.

2 Draw a circle for the mouth, and a tube-like shape for the body.

3 Add the antennae, face details, body, and tails. Ink over the final lines.

4 Erase any extra lines you do not need.

5 Add color and let's go see how the caterpillar becomes a butterfly!

MASAKI AND THE CATERPILLAR

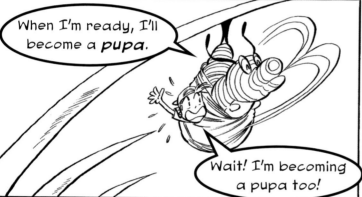

DRAWING A SCORPION

Let's make the scorpion a **villain**, since it has such a **poisonous sting!**

Begin by drawing an oval for the head.

1

Draw the body and tail. Don't forget the stinger at the end of the tail!

2

Add details to the face.

4

3

Add the two claws in front and the three pairs of legs along the body.

5

Ink over the lines you want to keep and erase the rest.

6

Now it's time to add color and then you're done! Let's go see what the scorpion gets up to!

DOCTOR SCORPION

DRAWING A LADYBUG

Let's draw a cute ladybug!

1 Draw a half circle for the body.

2 Draw two smaller half circles for the head.

3 Add the eyes and the legs.

4 Add the details to the body and face. Don't forget the dots on the back.

5 Ink over the final lines.

6 It's time to add color.

THE LADYBUG WAITRESS

DRAWING A
SPIDER

Just like the scorpion, the spider can be a villain, too. Let's start drawing!

Begin with a circle for the head.

1

2

Add an oval for the body.

3

Draw the *jaw*, antennae, and legs.

4

Add the rest of the details. Ink over the lines.

5

Erase any pencil lines you do not need.

6

When you're done coloring, let's follow the spider on his adventures.

A SPIDER'S TRAP

DRAWING A DRAGONFLY

Out of all the insects, I like the dragonfly the best. Let's draw one now!

1 Draw an oval for the dragonfly's head.

2 Add more ovals for the eyes and the chest. Draw a rectangle for the body.

3 Add the shapes shown for the wings.

Draw the legs. Look carefully at the drawing and add the details to the head and body.

4

5 Ink over the lines you want to keep and erase the rest.

6 Add any bright colors you would like to your dragonfly.

FLIGHT OF THE DRAGONFLY

DRAWING A
BUMBLEBEE

Bumblebees fly from flower to flower looking for **nectar**. Are you ready to draw the hungry bumblebee?

1. Start with an oval for the head.

2. Draw ovals for the neck, chest, and body.

3. Add ovals for the eyes and four more for the wings. Don't forget the legs!

4. Draw the antennae and other details. It's time to add ink.

5. Erase the extra pencil lines.

6. After coloring, let's go see what the bumblebee is up to!

BUMBLEBEE DANCE PARTY

GLOSSARY

amazing (uh-MAYZ-ing) Filling with wonder.

antennae (an-TEH-nee) Thin, rodlike feelers on the head of certain animals.

attraction (uh-TRAK-shun) Pulling something together or toward something else.

colony (KAH-luh-nee) A group that lives together.

comic books (KAH-mik BUHKS) Books with drawings that tell a story.

communicate (kuh-MYOO-nih-kayt) To share facts or feelings.

fashion (FA-shun) The latest clothes.

illustrate (IH-lus-trayt) To create pictures that help explain a story, poem, or book.

injection (in-JEKT-shun) Using a sharp object to force something into a body.

inspiration (in-spuh-RAY-shun) Powerful, moving guidance.

jaw (JAH) Bones in the top and bottom of the mouth.

larvae (LAHR-vee) Animals in the early life period in which they have a wormlike form.

medicine (MEH-duh-sin) A drug that a doctor gives you to help fight illness.

nectar (NEK-tur) A sweet liquid found in flowers.

plots (PLOTS) The events that happen in a story.

poisonous (POYZ-nus) Causing pain or death.

popular (PAH-pyuh-lur) Liked by lots of people.

protecting (pruh-TEKT-ing) Keeping safe.

pupa (PYOO-puh) The second stage of life for an insect, in which it changes from a larva to an adult.

sketch (SKECH) A quick drawing.

sting (STING) Pain caused by an animal using a sharp part to hurt another animal.

text (TEKST) The words in a piece of writing.

unique (yoo-NEEK) One of a kind.

villain (VI-len) A wicked or evil person.

Meet the Insects!

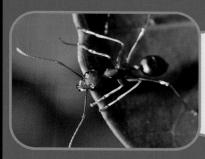

Ants
are social insects that form colonies so that they can work together for the common good.

Ladybugs
are generally considered a "cute" insect and are a favorite of children.

Butterflies
are known for their beautiful colors and for their unusual life cycles.

Spiders
produce silk, which they use to spin webs in order to trap food.

Caterpillars
are the larval stage of the butterfly's life cycle. They will soon turn into butterflies!

Dragonflies
are normally found near water. They eat mosquitoes and other small insects.

Scorpions
have stingers with poisonous venom. Luckily, this venom is usually harmless to people.

Bumblebees
are larger and furrier than other bees. They are normally gentle insects that do not sting often.

INDEX